Rembrandt Would
Have Loved You

RUTH PADEL

REMBRANDT WOULD HAVE LOVED YOU

REMBRANDT WOULD HAVE LOVED YOU

Ruth Padel

Chatto & Windus
LONDON

Published by Chatto & Windus 1998

2 4 6 8 10 9 7 5 3

Copyright © Ruth Padel 1998

Ruth Padel has asserted her right under the Copyright, Designs
and Patents Act 1988 to be identified as the author of this work

First published in Great Britain in 1998 by
Chatto & Windus
Random House, 20 Vauxhall Bridge Road,
London SW1V 2SA

Random House Australia (Pty) Limited
20 Alfred Street, Milsons Point, Sydney,
New South Wales 2061, Australia

Random House New Zealand Limited
18 Poland Road, Glenfield,
Auckland 10, New Zealand

Random House South Africa (Pty) Limited
Endulini, 5A Jubilee Road, Parktown 2193, South Africa

Random House UK Limited Reg. No. 954009

A CIP catalogue record for this book
is available from the British Library

ISBN 0 7011 67157

Papers used by Random House UK Limited are natural,
recyclable products made from wood grown in sustainable forests.
The manufacturing processes conform to the environmental
regulations of the country of origin.

Typeset by Deltatype Ltd, Birkenhead, Merseyside
Printed and bound in Great Britain by
Mackays of Chatham PLC

For Colm Tóibín

*

It is human nature to stand in the middle of a thing
But you cannot stand in the middle of this . . .

Marianne Moore

CONTENTS

ACKNOWLEDGEMENTS

Thanks to the editors of the following, where versions of some of these poems appeared: *The Devil, Forward Poetry – Book of the Year 1996, From the Window, Harvard Review, The Independent, London Magazine, London Review of Books, Making for Planet Alice* (edited by Maura Dooley), *Navis, New Writing 6* (edited by A. S. Byatt and Peter Porter), *The New Yorker, The North, The Observer, Paralos, Poetry London Newsletter, P.N. Review, Poetry Review, Shenandoah, Southern Humanities Review, Tabla, Thumbscrew, Verse.*

'Icicles Round a Tree in Dumfriesshire' was winner of the 1996 National Poetry Competition.

'Easter Candle' was first broadcast on *Best Words*, BBC Radio 3.

Many warm thanks for criticism to Jo, Don, Elaine, Andrew, Myles, Dermot, Jonathan Burnham and especially Matthew Sweeney.

ICICLES ROUND A TREE IN
DUMFRIESSHIRE

We're talking different kinds of vulnerability here.
　These icicles aren't going to last for ever
Suspended in the ultraviolet rays of a Dumfries sun.
　But here they hang, a frozen whirligig of lightning,
And the famous American sculptor
　Who scrambles the world with his tripod
For strangeness *au naturel*, got sunset to fill them.
　It's not comfortable, a double helix of opalescent fire

Wrapping round you, swishing your bark
　Down cotton you can't see,
On which a sculptor planned his icicles,
　Working all day for that Mesopotamian magic
Of last light before the dark
　In a suspended helter-skelter, lit
By almost horizontal rays:
　Making a mist-carousel from the House of Diamond,

A spiral of Pepsodent darkening to the shadowfrost
　Of cedars at the Great Gate of Kiev.
Why it makes me think of opening the door to you
　I can't imagine. No one could be less
Of an icicle. But there it is –
　Having put me down in felt-tip
In the mystical appointment book,
　You shoot that quick

Inquiry-glance, head tilted, when I open up,
　Like coming in's another country,
A country you want but have to get used to, hot
　From your *bal masqué*, making sure
That what you found before's
　Still here: a spiral of touch and go,
Lightning licking a tree
　Imagining itself Aretha Franklin

I

Singing 'You make me feel like a natural woman'
  In *basso profondo*,
Firing the bark with its otherworld ice
  The way you fire, lifting me
Off my own floor, legs furled
  Round your trunk as that tree goes up
At an angle inside the lightning, roots in
  The orange and silver of Dumfries.

Now I'm the lightning now you, you are,
  As you pour yourself round me
Entirely. No who's doing what and to who,
  Just a tangle of spiral and tree.
You might wonder about sculptors who come all this way
  To make a mad thing that won't last.
You know how it is: you spend a day, a whole life.
  Then the light's gone, you walk away

To the Galloway Paradise Hotel. Pine-logs,
  Cutlery, champagne – OK,
But the important thing was making it.
  Hours, and you don't know how it'll be.
Then something like light
  Arrives last moment, at speed reckoned
Only by horizons: completing, surprising
  With its three hundred thousand

Kilometres per second.
  Still, even lightning has its moments of panic.
You don't get icicles catching the midwinter sun
  In a perfect double helix in Dumfriesshire every day.
And can they be good for each other,
  Lightning and tree? It'd make anyone,
Wouldn't it, afraid? That rowan would adore
  To sleep and wake up in your arms

But's scared of getting burnt.
    And the lightning might ask, touching wood,
'What do you want of me, now we're in the same
    Atomic chain?' What can the tree say?
'Being the centre of all that you are to yourself –
    That'd be OK. Being my own body's fine
But it needs yours to stay that way.'
    No one could live for ever in

A suspended gleam-on-the-edge,
    As if sky might tear any minute.
Or not for ever for long. Those icicles
    Won't be surprise any more.
The little snapped threads
    Blew away. Glamour left that hill in Dumfries.
The sculptor went off with his black equipment.
    Adzes, twine, leather gloves.

What's left is a photo
    Of a completely solitary sight
In a book anyone can open.
    And whether our touch at the door gets forgotten
Or turned into other sights, light, form,
    I hope you'll be truthful
To me. At least as truthful as lightning,
    Skinning a tree.

FALLING

This isn't happening

Play it down
Dress it in Levis or a babygro

Buy it a hamburger
Buy it a drink

Put it out with the cat
Make a credit card arrangement
With the taxidermist on Upper Street

Book it a package deal
Where icicles go

For their holiday in spring
This isn't happening

And it's doing it so fast.

THE CLEARING

Someone has brushed the pale grass-heads the wrong way
Over the haunches of the hills. They stare fluffily up,
  A continuous Saluki against these sweeps of chalk
Saying 'sumptuous', 'ancient', everywhere you look.
We'll follow them. Through an empty cottage garden

That'd do for *Peter Rabbit* or the Annunciation –
All lily-pots, waiting on winter –
  Over cowpats, barbed wire, kissing-stile
To the hidden river, glass heart of the valley
With its mystical silvery cows.

We fetch up in a hide of nettles, our chapel
In the forest. Green priests splashing
  Leaf-filtered sun
On my hair, my throat, your shoulders and spine –
Whichever part of the two of us combines to be uppermost –

Then melting it down
In shallows by the bank. How could I know I'd find
  You here, on a film-set
By Chrétien de Troyes – you who never stop
Talking except when your mouth is on mine?

7

THE EYES

When he came down from the platform
And walked out,
Everyone clapping,

His eyes as he passed her were proud
Shy of being proud

And glad she was there.
She was a lightning photographer
Handed the secret of storms.

Think iridescent. After all the myth stuff
  Of meeting, of coming alive,
We both hit the road. The journey back unfolds
What the down train never showed –

That Tintagel-look-alike castle,
  Not there, I swear, first time round.
To our right, a new-minted sea
Flashes its Book of Hours cerulean

Over British Rail Chicken Tikka Massala,
  Surprising the triple-glazing
With its hug of open gold. The Darley Arabian
In person, sire of racing legend, the original

Snow-thoroughbred, is looking our way
  As if Lancelot caught his steed on polaroid
Before he mounted him,
Then pasted the enlargement on a hill.

Those Druids (think of the mistletoe) – someone
  Had railways and lovers in mind
When they chalked out this boy's stamping-ground.
He's a master of desire, giving the high sign

To our remit into the waking world
  Made newleaf-green as Malory, or the lyre of Iggy Pop.
Also to you beside me, sleepy, almost already
A part of me, turning my skin to fire.

... and it isn't I believe I'm irresistible,

Very far from it, Jesus,
But when every cell

[*Something dropped out here, the paper*
Feels brittle,
Stained with a splash]

In my body aches
To touch you, why do you drape yourself round
Every woman in the room?

And [*something else missing, maybe a dash,*
Or something with F in it]
Where do you find

A taxi in this part of town?

As they listened in the Musicians' Gallery
To jesters and tall stories
He could smell cumin from her curry a mile off
And his breathing had a hotline to her breasts.

It could have been Beowulf himself down there
Sounding off in the Great Hall
Where butterflies swept through stone windows
Making the moment a lifetime

Of tremble and glide. They knew then
They would fall on each other by the small
Window's leaded diamonds
Where if they'd had time to look

They'd have seen
A smocking of stars, blue cedars of Lebanon,
Velvet lawns brushed by a Sorcerer's Moon
Which came in to light the bare duvet.

Darkness. For the first time you hear
The body that has made itself core
Of the universe (or anyway, you reckon now,
Of yours), slacken its guy-ropes for sleep

As if mile-deep water
Were slap-settling round you in a lake
Whose speedboat carnivals, much as you adored
The show they made, have gone.

It's a website of alien muscles
Losing their hair-trigger touch on a soul
Blowing Christ knows where. This is all
New. But you say

(To him, to yourself),
I'll follow, if you give the sign.

THE HILL

Hard to tell if it was the world or you,
The warmth that held us, all that sailing
Sunlight, going back. As if we were at home,
It was our hill, you pulled the photo

Of your children from your jacket. Beautiful.
And said, 'He's just like me. As I was.'
Gold sky, green before the autumn. Tilt

Of the horizon. Everything at a different angle
Rolling on its camber. Everything we wanted
Found, like rivers and being alone.
Hard to tell
If the magic was you, that photo, or the land.

UNDRESSING

... as if you'd won me at a fair,
A five-foot-seven, willow-patterned vase,
For some great blokeish dare –
Ringing the bell

In a weight-smashing blow
Or banging away with a rifle
At cut-outs of Camilla and Charles –
Then carried me

Through candyfloss and frogpool stalls,
The Teacups Roundabout, the Water Chute,
The gipsy gold-and-rainbow
Double-decker carousel –

My thoughtless love
Not so thoughtless this moment though –
As if I were true-blue Venetian glass
And no one else to carry me would do.

BED-TIME

Time to go to bed again. Time for the moon
To get in among the muddle of arms and legs,
  Get completely unstrung and set free
  And hold on to you. Because you've done
All this but are also the one thing
That'll hold me, lost in this narrow room

As if it's Pharaoh's mine of slippery agate,
  Flashing quartz chambers
Where I could wander for years

Now changed to an arch of green cedars
And a wild-honey garden of mist and secret walks
  With cyclamen in the shade, a tiltyard
  Of tiered lawns rising and rising – to sundials, mazes
And driftwood igloos seeing off dew from their walls
At dawn. Because of you. Because of you.

That God-is-Light smile of your arms
One second before
I'm in them.

Your eyes, having nearly
Given up, lit up
As mythical

As Regent Street. A satyr
Reeling at the discovery of honey.
Your mouth,

Tasting of the breath
Of greenhouses. The sap.
The open stamens. Chlorophyll.

. . . full of things I long
To give you. Grapefruit trees in bloom.
A giant elmwood bowl reminding me –
That go-ahead grain, the way it opens
To the world – of you. An antique map
Of where you're from. A photograph of Beckett.
I could go on
For ever. That wild beaked mask from Venice,
Gold on black, all carnival –
And a tasselled Iznik sword.

A sword! Your son
Would buzz with that one all his life.
He'd ask to touch it, hanging in your room,
And love the getting awed – the tip,
Its memories, those stained-plum velvet pads
In the embossed sheath. How you'd adore
Taking it down,
Releasing it – full-blooded,
Ceremonious – for him. How he'd inherit it
And say, 'This was my dad's.'

ECHO

If (you say, pre-empting things, when you call
The evening off)
*Arrangements go the least bit wrong
You make a fuss: 'I've been stood up!'*

It's been three weeks. But there's your career
To think of.
I mind, I say, not seeing you.
How sweet, you murmur. *Oh – me too.*

My this month's gift to you
   Tips chemicals down my throat each day –
A pill, clogging linings and arteries,
Bloodcells, breath. For days whose nights you fill
With, let's say, Sam.

O cabaret! O parties! There's no way
   You'd opt for an evening here
Instead. You break my sleep
And something like my heart. Still,
I'd rather have the pain

Of being 'understanding' yet again, than do like you
   (Or as I feel, just now, you do): pretend.
Excuse. Burst people's lives apart
With charm. I can't do much about it.
Can't, for instance, take another pill,

Loading my lungs with pharmaceuticals *ad nauseam*
   Each morning, to conjure Roman virtue
(Integrity, say) in you. I'd like to think
That if I could, I wouldn't. But I would,
I gladly would. Despite the world called Sam.

Watching him handle his life as a flame-thrower
  On pilgrimage
For a key geological event –

Say, volcanic eruption in snow,
  The frozen cocaine of church bells
Giving out under ice below Reykjavik –

Or let's say he's something more animate,
  A very endangered species of tiger,
The kind that makes himself go

Without silence, not giving stillness a chance
  On his fire-clawed search to be loved,
Crying at Disney,

Not seeming always to like himself much
  But giving his tiger-all
To whatever's on hand at the moment,

You worry,
  Seeing him glitter out that ruthless
Innocent blaze (does a tiger need to be moral?)

Rushing at everything:
  What will he have of his own
At the jungle's end?

No one found the penguins odd in Crete.
They were standing around there silent,
  The way penguins do, in my sleep
(With a job-lot of seals playing 'Tango for Marsha'
In headphones and quiffs): on the rocks, flipper-calm,
  Absolutely at home
With their backdrop of blue-bitten islands
Each promising something of their own
But holding, as islands have to,

Separate secrets close to their cliffs.
Cork Airport. We rented a Datsun
  Under the rainbow. The dysfunctional clutch
Had long gone, but here we all were, a T-junction
Near Dalkey on the Gulf of Mirabello
  (Billie Holiday burning away on
The tape deck), hunting for somebody's
High-heeled shoe. Someone of yours – a woman
I didn't know, was afraid of – her gold slipper lost

In a Titan-size telly. We got shown
The famous precipice of indigo
  And amethyst. But I woke on my own
To the first train of morning, a bubble of you
At the end of my throat
  Where tonsils would be if I had them,
Whisking me back
To an evening on ocean-blue
Floorboards, cheek to the cliff of your belly.

MISTY

How I love

The darkwave music
Of a sun's eclipse
You can't see for cloud

The saxophonist playing 'Misty'
In the High Street outside Barclays

Accompanied by mating-calls
Sparked off
In a Jaguar alarm

The way you're always there
Where I'm thinking

Or several beats ahead.

HEATWAVE

I could stand on the mountain's tip,
  Snow-winds dancing their socks off
At eight hundred kilometres a minute,
Frost on all the outer trim
Of whatever winterkit is *de rigueur*
  These days in that aeolian pitch
Of seamless grit from outer space,

And if my body were wrapped in mainly yours
  You'd recognise
Among the wind-raked snowcaps
This same surprise skin-flame, amps flowing
In directions I hadn't known about before
  Towards those bitten-back sighs
You make, like you'd been alone for years.

There'd be heatwave on Everest
  Plus that weird relief
Of bodies becoming each other's journey's end
Or seeing bees swarm in your own apple trees
And a helical slipstream of woodpigeons bend
  In a clear domestic fashion
Down the mountain, home.

I'd like to be what you believe in
As you hammer through your whirlpool of a week.
   Don't want to be with you in all that
Hadn't bargained for parties
   Don't want to see how they end
But I'd like to keep
The way I stood in your warmth on the platform

Bound by invisible cord
Which turns out to be not so damn invisible
   When I spill into your gravitational field,
A flying bit of vertical velcro,
   A planet yawed from its orbit
And headed for land. Despite the dizziness
I'd like to hang on to that physics,

These molecules
Whirling their partners through
   The magnetism waltz, as a stone
I touch in my pocket secretly, alone.
   I'd love to think you'd keep it too.
I'd like to be what you believe in
As I believe (unlikely as it sounds) in you.

So you think I don't give a toss
How you work your ass off?
    Hmmm. It's in me all the time, plus
Other looking-after stuff
I can't keep my mind free of,

Like how if you crashed your Toyota
Going home, through exhaustion and drink
    Or came down with parapneumonia
In some BUPA hospital? Who would I phone,
What would I do?

Think I'm incapable of caring about you
At the end of your week,
    Fifteen-month baby flopped sideways to sleep
On your lap, Spice Girls doing 'Wannabe' lullabies
Through the CD as she hitches and wraps

Herself deeper, twitching in sleep
Like fur on a spaniel dreaming of hunting,
    And radiating that velveteen-felt heat
Till *your* muscles melt
To the heaviness I know, and you're asleep too,

Your head flopping down over hers against the wall?
As I used to fall, sitting up into sleep with mine –
    Who now curls, a heap
Of *Saddle Club* pony books, under my bedclothes,
But used to latch unconscious on a nipple every night.

Everything outside, even my own skin, cold,
But that was the centre, that hearth-ember sleep
    You hold until you share it, as if you're incomplete
Without the borrowed heat
Of flame-resistant flannelette, that soft-breath rubato.

Part of me is sure you must deserve
All I can throw at you, and more.
The rest of me believes you're thoughtless, yes,
But also anxious, loving, seven skins too few
And so – so unaware you make me weep.
You never see the choice I see you making
Week by week. Your hunting song
In geisha city taking pride of place.
(Or am I wrong?) As if there's something in you
That had never had enough,
You've had to keep on seeking. Pan in love
With a green elusive Echo, her not-yet face
Embalming his. A recidivist lemon sherbert,
Depending on exposure to the public air, for fizz.

We're different species. Never mind the odd unkind
Reproach: you give me what a river gives a city –
A heartline for the palm of a closed-in hand.
Despite these shadowed banks (bloodclots
Tadpoling about through sagging veins,
The priest knifed at communion, bitter dying words
To a frightened wife) it's all here, all of it again,
And lifting when you're on the bridge.
You suddenly remember – Augustine to Hollywood –
Just what a city is. This human going-on at being grand.
The sea directive darkling at its centre, hung
With necklaces of light. Different ways
Of knowing, flowing within my own. Like you.
Like you again. The generous night.

SCOTCH

The fox you didn't know you had
In your front garden
  Is craning his velour neck
From the hedge at two in the morning
To see what he doesn't often get a glimpse of,

That moonspark
  On a glass of Scotch
He doesn't often smell

Being more at home with fish-heads
And the rinds of Emmental:
  Identifying, to his fox-astonishment,
A tumbler doing the rounds of his own beat
About heart-height in the dark.

... kissed me in my own garden
Under shadow-ripples

Of four apple trees
In fruit

And diamond trellis
All leaves and lattice on tough grass

Backlit from a million high-rise
Yellow windows,

Saying, How do you like –
Like being in a shadow pagoda –

How do you like the breeze
On your nipples?

If sleep's what you're short of
I'll do a deal with God about a day and night
 To let you have it here. Let your eyes close
On all the small beer junk
Around this room. The pomegranates
 Blown from ruby glass. The fathomless
CD player, William Morris brown and blue
Convolvulus and dogrose
My granny sewed together (clumsily, like me)

For blackout curtains. Plus the card I've kept
On mantelpieces, windowsills and bathroom shelves
 For years,
And now see why –
Of Tutankhamun's alabaster cup
 Which promises he'll face the rising sun
Looking happiness smack in the eye.
Hope of forever. Hope in a cup,
Of a future

When tentative faxes, crazily late
Late nights, pissed failures
 To be together alone
Will never matter. What a con,
This Pharaoh,
 Trying to bribe history like that,
Trying to go one better than he got.
Whoever made the thing for him was better off.
Who wouldn't be glad

To have made it? Look at it, translucent
Before windows were invented,
   Shadowed with the veiny bloom
Of half-skimmed milk. If you're not asleep,
Not yet, look closer. Lotus-petals, fanned
   In chalky rainbows round the side,
Make you want to cup it, slide your cheek down
Soft along it,
Weigh it, very gently, in your hand.

CLEARING UP

When I'm afraid of being swept away
And wrap myself into your shoulder
Muttering 'Look after me, a bit', the bloke
Part of you takes it

As a meta-Spice-Girls joke. But then
I find me swabbing the New World Grill
With tears, while you keep saying you
Don't want another child. 'Think' – you go on,

And on, and on – 'of the practicalities'.
I try for 'Don't be daft – I told you, I
Don't either,' but the words won't graft
Themselves to me. Won't sort.

Who are you calling practicalities, anyway?
I count them, worry about their feelings,
Every day. What a time he'd have, poor bugger,
Getting up their noses. How I'd get stuck

And muddled. But you invented him, this son,
Saying 'Could you? Could we?'
Imagining how he'd look, cracking him up
Like life insurance, sales-talking what he'd do

For me: would rake my heart (why put it
Like that, I wonder?) but maybe think,
Years later, he'd done something wrong.
'Because you asked', I tell the sink

(Scouring as if the J-cloth's life
Depended on it), 'I wanted to say goodbye
To all of that. Say it carefully. With you.'
But the night's gone quicksand as you talk.

I'm sitting at the dentist's in an earthquake.
The guy can't keep his eye
Still, let alone his hand.
But the pain's not his. I've given my heart

To something I need protection from.
An autistic dodgem on a windy day.
A hobnailed boot
Who adores being catered for

And understood, one-way.
Who's into surfaces, the glitter
On his cake. Who'd win a blue
For ballroom ruthlessness.

He came to the church bazaar
With its nightclub floor-polish aura
   And slammed his fist
On the pew top's open glitter
   Demanding his due –

Expenses, free pass,
Press pack, recognition.
   He was asked his licence number.
Draughts rustled
   Through the woman-on-the-door's paper bag.

This is the life I paid for.
'But where's the tenderness
   We ordered for you? What's this score
Of other people's scars,
   This lifelong love affair

With words you never meant
One moment to the next –
   All the effects
Without the thing itself?'
   Checking the computer:

'What've you done
With the warmgold heart we tailor-made?
   We don't give those away
To everyone. You've become
   A master of dis-

Appointment, disregard.
A cliff-wall up the long
   Estuary where the sea
Runs sailors up so fast
   They crash the doom-bar.'

Look at her. Danaë in
   A mostly darkness world, top hip aseethe
With light, watching the curtain, naked, for that zoom

Of homing gold. You know you'll cock this up,
   Whatever's coming, but keep the curtain open to
The metalwork invasion. Hoofprints off the moon.

Here for a short, a shadow time, we light
   Each other up, defined
By what we're vulnerable to. In my case, you –

A lion whose brass paws flash in the plain,
   That sudden dash of sea-fire
When a sleeping wave rolls over in the harbour

In the night. Secrets of your body, filed
   In mine. A harvest-time.
Your woken-tungsten smile.

SISTERS

Why should the iron scrollwork
  Over windows
In this Islington-Byzantine church

Where we're listening to Mary Black
  And downing St Patrick's wine from plastic cups,
So sing to me of you?

I'm here in my life. You're elsewhere
  In yours. The whole thing's clear.
I'm fine. But all this over-wrought

Victorian iron
  (That writhing flow and curl
Rock-hard against the night)

Won't let me be. It goes on shouting so
  Embarrassingly, vividly of you,
I'm frightened. Women will get to know.

The ones all round me, all these *Guardian*
  Journalists: why don't they rise
In a body, bellowing *j'accuse*?

Quite frightening, this delight
  In being filled and lifted, anything –
You name it, *anything* – by you.
  Then seeing you in so much public,
Half-way down
  A staircase from the glove-and-thunder
Ballroom parts of *War and Peace*,

Being domestic
  With that concentrated looking-after look
As if not treading on new grass,
  The way I guess you look at children
When they're tired and cross –
  That whiny shiver when a child
Refuses anything so unperceiving
  As a parent. ('Tired? *Tired*? Not *me*.')

Your gentlest side. Suddenly
  There's a whole new load on board.
Love for whoever you look after,
  And – what *is* this? – loving you more
For it. Easy to say. I can glance
  Through someone else's banisters,
Pick up my coat, my scarf,
  Zebra a path through offers of lifts
I'll never need, and drive away.

Entirely the right reaction, I'd have thought,
To hum that song
  Along Southampton Row
Taking your new-shorn silverpaper hair
And wariness I didn't know about
En route to me.

When your body's whole menagerie
Breaks out under my hands in sweat
  And you look in me as though
The world stopped here,
'Smoke Gets in Your Eyes' is not a patch
On us. Like we opened the bathroom cabinet

Looking for paracetamol, and found
A flying foal. An equine angel, ivory heart aglow
  But slippery-cool to touch
As the card round your parents' photo.
I can't forget it.
His hand over hers, about to cut the cake.

Two champagne glasses, close together,
Empty. Her eyes into the camera,
  Full face. And yours,
With that round-the-corner glint
Inviting me to blush in French
Or share some what-have-I-done-this-time joke,

Flashing sideways out of his:
That grown-up-tom-kitten glance
  Your son looked out of too,
  Askance, in his Christmas play.
While five-year-old kings in Smarties coronets
Were taking photo calls, Joseph

Was whisking Mary away,
Arm round her tinsel shoulder,
  For Beaujolais Nouveau
In some little-known Bethlehem dive.
You, when you look aside,
Look straight from the heart. I know,

Don't worry. Watching you calm down and see
Yourself in me, tears me apart. Catch it in
  The Faber Book of Fortune-Telling –
All the lymph-cells in my body ache
Imagining how empty
Your corral will feel if you let me go.

A BIT OF A WELCOME

Days after you go,
Your ghost is still with her. Green-pullovered,
   Laughing about the house. Never mind that her phone
   Can catch you a sea away now,
   There's still a son, a you
Pouring whisky, filling her home; and talking,
Talking all day.

But which does she want? The you on the phone?
Or Christmas you, miraculously heavy in her chair,
   Laying your head in her lap – 'The way',
   She says, 'you used'? She almost can't care,
   But wishes one of you
Had someone to come home to
Who'd give him a bit of a welcome:

The kind she's had in her head for centuries,
Heartbeat warm
   For that man
   Coming in from the sea, the building site,
   The long stone road.
Proud of you, wishing you happy,
She stands beside you in the mirror

Twice your age exactly now, and shocks you sideways
Wishing you and she were married.
   Maybe, she thinks, that'd do.
   I watch you go from my door
   To the new year's morning snow,
And know how she feels, ghosthaunting
And all. The wanting to give

And wanting you back. The confusion
Of two of you. The disappearing car –
   And that phantom
   Cluttering the bedroom, kitchen, hearth.
   The folksong called Not-Here-
Most-of-the-Time. The smack
Of the long stone path.

The sunken harbour bulbs, their summer shapes
   Of dolphins, smugglers, killer whales,
Are all turned out. A black sea sushi-bars
   Its wildly out-of-season secrets
Only to us. The empty restaurant fades
Its *dolce vita* tape, to let us sing.

We do 'After the Ball Is Over',
   'The Ballad of Abdul Abulbul Amir',
Plus things I truffle-hunted as a child
   Through *The Penquin Songbook*'s
Furry sellotape. Those songs were my discovery,
I thought. The first thing that was mine:

Thanks to Miss Lewin from Jamaica
   Who despaired of me on piano
But at the end of every Saraband
   And Concertina, played
For me to try them out,
Those little songs. Then headed back

To her own songs, her island, with a man.
   Who, like the guy
In 'Allen Water', left her
   To raise a daughter (murder and politics
Flickering all round her), start a choir
In prison. Disappear.

Tonight the mystery-Scots, those other-country,
   Once-my-country words, come rushing back
With 'Sweet the lavrock's note and lang'.
   (His *lang?* Does every lavrock
Have one?) That Bonnie Charlie song
I sang alone for years –

For the tune, for missing things,
    For infant rage at empire
(Jeez, that was just the beginning) –
    For whatever that song gave.
But all those years, you say
In the light of our final

Cinnamon candle, your father
    Was singing it too. Tonight
And ever after
    It's a song for the harbour,
For the tears in your eyes.
The song you cut on his grave.

Some day (I tell myself) you might
   Take down this book,
   Not to show a woman – although that
Is certain to be in there too – but to remember.

Then perhaps (I can't be sure) you'll hear
   The longing, the wanting to pour
The whole world out before you,

For you. The fugue of held-in hurt
   At your not phoning, cancelling,
Not wanting to imagine what's got felt

As long as I didn't complain.
   The chaos you're so good at,
And promises so brilliantly forgotten.

And ask, Did I do that? Did I really not know
   What I heard, since I could misinterpret it
   At the drop of every hat? What else
Was so important that I let that go?

Thank God we cast
A spot of shadow in our lives,
　Said the *Mahabharata* bride,
Facing five versions of her groom –

Your man himself plus four male gods,
Four dead-spit images, self-xeroxed in his shape –
　Who recognised that heartbeat,
The man she'd have to part with,

By the shadow at his heel. Gods don't go round
Casting shadow. Things *we* do and feel
　(As a leader in *The Independent*
Put it afterwards) are incomplete.

This is innocent. Teenage. Blossom
Without leaf. It's not a gun.
Not threatening anyone's conservatory,
Private school, or bank account.

Lies are being kept to a minimum
And lives are going on as they always have
And shall. We're only Noël Coward,
Lightest of light tenors, percolating

'Fate has sent me you'
Through the cherry-snow of Russell Square;
A hedgehog star of icicles lit
By the sun's last rays on the lip of a cliff.

The song will end,
The whole thing fall to pieces, when
We get to the forbidden mountain's heart.
It'll all be known. There'll be iron

With its cruel ideas. And maybe I'll stop
Saying the 'Our Father' in that narrow space
Between the bath and sweat-foxed
Mirror, hugging a towel

And thanking Someone, Anything,
For you. Morality. A trapdoor spider's
Inner web. A tinderbox. Where we are
Has no answers.

STILL LIFE WITH LOAVES, SEAWEED AND WREN

Whatever self is, I'd like mine to wake up with yours
While sleep is still plumping the skin,
Warm bread rising gently in the oven.
   An enamel oven, opened on a summer morning
In a village in Provence
By a woman who's never been unkind, whose children
And husband and lover have never been hurt.
   It's not that real a place,

I do know that. But for this moment of waking
I'm imagining, it holds
The warmest small patisserie in the world
   Which does its baking in a sloping village street
By the wall of the local château.
Relations with that château have always been brilliant.
There was no need for revolution, there wasn't one.
   It's all been OK, that side of things.

There are baguettes in the baguette corner
As there have been two hundred years
And will go on being, for in this village
   No worlds end. Light pours down the little street
With all promise of a hot day to come
But not yet, not yet. A street in which no girl
Has been ungenerous to her lover,
   No child mown down by alcoholic lorries,

No resistance fighter shot. And no Jew shopped
By neighbours who wanted his farm.
The Cathars and the Huguenots were fine.
   I'm going to reel back history for these bakers,
Map them on the road to Eden. Children will come in
For *pain au chocolat* and get it free.
Parents will come
   For newspapers, milk and a gossip

Which never knifes anyone in the back, not really,
And sun will spread through the doorway
Without alarming the profiterolles,
  Their glisten of chocolate, that delicate cream.
This stove is Delphi, navel of the world,
There's you and me in it, and maybe some other
Lucky loaves, expanding their crusts
  For the day, to mutter 'We're together, it's OK'.

And if other sorts of loaf, seedcake or sparbunkle,
Think it all sounds pretty boring lying there –
Loom-weights in a loaf-museum, none of the mica-sparkle
  Of the scythe – they can fuck off elsewhere.
For whatever self is, I'd like mine to wake with yours,
Curls mixing on the pillow surprised – as if, seconds before,
The separate hairs weren't calcium and follicles
  But sweeping off on some quite different enterprise

Of being. Maybe hair dreams of being dandelion seed
Blown over rivers, gold forests, the motorway *du sol*.
These curls of ours can do that. Let them go helium-ballooning,
  Linked very lightly, as far as they want.
Or maybe they'd like to be seaweed
At the bottom of an East Aegean bay, swaying their tips
In sky-water whose ripples you can't see, only feel,
  A virtual reality of movement that gets the weeds excited

Very gently. A pure bit of sea, *naturellement*,
None of your oil slicks and rubbish from foreign yachts.
Yes, if the hairs want to have been that, they can,
  Then be glad to come back to us, as we wake
In this bakery whose warmth is not electronic but self-made.
The loaves created it. They'd like to stay all day
Half-dreaming they are apples in a loft, radiating Cézanne,
  Dapple-lit by a window so old it is ouzo,

Quite certain no roof will ever fall. No one visits them
Except a child, who'll remember all her life
The smell, the soft still light with dust along its spine,
   The silent, consenting apples.
Yet whatever selves are, I'd like mine to wake
And not only dream
With yours. Be risen loaves, not fixing to get eaten
   But to get their act together.

Loaves that are going to give themselves names
And float out into the world
Looking like people who get phoned up,
   Arrange meetings and deadlines, difficult lunches.
They'll be separate loaves paying their own bills
But all day in their soft loaf parts
Keep a patch of themselves away
   Where they woke up touching –

As a wren, I imagine, keeps the impress of eggs
Left hidden in her penny-size nest
When she darts out shopping, through the teeth
   Of hawthorn, for her list of things she needs.
Mayfly. Lacewing. And there they stay,
Those six-millimetre ovals, pressed
In the faint fawn-feather of her breast.
   No harm's coming to her or the eggs,

Nothing broken or planning to break. No need for a wren
To say sorry, or suffer anything but the warm spark
Of morning, dawn-hunts among buds of Russian vine
   For that greenfly tickle on her tiny wren tongue
And the mercy of having woken touching
What she loves. Whatever love is for a wren.
And whatever self is, I'd like yours to wake,
   If it wouldn't mind, with mine.

Shadows don't gather up your flowered skirt
After lifting it over your head,
Don't kiss it, bury their face in it,
   Lay it softly on the bed. Catch a shadow
Slipping its hand
Inside your shirt – so gently, first,

A swarm of adoring bees
Comes winding round your breast,
Making another skin, another mind
   In which you live for this,
Only to be the place of rest
And homecoming for this one man.

You don't have baths with shadows.
They never sing. And when they lift
You to the draining board
   For a higher level kiss
You don't feel you've been given
The world's whole history of gift.

The nerve of me! To think 'protect'
At anything so separate and whole
As you. Look at me, face down –

You cover me entirely
And some over. There's nothing I could do
To guard this flesh of yours, nearly

But not quite crushing me into the sheets
Then scooping me into its arms
And drifting bear-asleep all round me,

As if a puma wrapped a child
In a velvet-collared coat
To keep her safe all winter.

But aren't I where you've stowed the keys to caves
Where dreams that made you you
Got made? They've found a home

In whatever earth I am, indelible
As indigo in linen
Or the raggedy smoke cross

Burnt on the lintel, in the name
Of safe and keeping,
By the Easter candle's resurrection-flame.

MAN TRYING TO UNITE HIS LIFE WITH
A SCRATCHED CD

So selfish, always wanting you to stay.
Wish it was me who had to drive
   Through thirteen million sleeping Londoners
   As you will, in a moment. But you're still here,
Annoyed with a CD
Your children play all day,

Whirling its difficult silver
In my machine, refusing to obey
   The proper button. You can't know
   How scattered saffron
From the bedside bulb
Is doing you proud, chiaroscuroing

Your chin, your belly, flowing
Its hands and tongue
   Up the inside of your arms.
   Meniscuses of light –
Floods and feathers of the stuff –
Welling on every inch of skin

And nesting milky on your shoulder
Like the smoky blush on silk
   Where the muscle's rounding in
   Towards your chest. Rembrandt would have loved
That cross intensity, naked against the dark.
And so much dark, all round.

He'd have brushed shadow
How the hairs grow, down
   The inside of your thighs
   And made this candled moment sing
Of a life we'll never live together,
The way he made his mother –

That book so close to her eyes –
Spell out how difficult it is to see
    The things we love
    With all this shadow round us,
This brief time we're here.
He'd have seen darkness

Love you like the light, and me.
And called it 'Man trying to unite
    His life with a scratched CD'.
    I want to make a formal thing of it
And hold it as I can't hold you
For ever. The tiny Safeways bulb

Making a shell of light for us like faith.
How you stand facing a song that won't be fished
    To land from its silver pool.
    How I'm washed with love for every cell
Of what's in front of me,
That *Gentleman's Relish* irritation

I'll never see full blast in a home of mine.
We're just the awestruck leopards
    Who turn up in the temple on a visit,
    Watershine
Playing over edges of domestic dark,
An *ignis fatuus* blown through copper smoke.

Or lightning, spooling its sharp white honey
In the earth. We're all this fine,
    But we're not a house. Rembrandt's caught us
    In a moment that's not ours,
A break from being lightning. You wanted to lie
Beside me, bathing in this music, and the bloody thing

Won't work. It's human to hold on to what you love,
Even when it's got to put on boxer shorts
   And roar away through London. It's male to get
   Exasperated with CDs that don't fall
Quivering into line. And female, any rate here
And now, to let that fury wring me to the core.

Things happen so quickly between us
    And when I see you cross
There's also that female thing

Of trying to calm horses. Look,
    The mustang's wounded, or he thinks he is,
By gun, lasso and overwork. By stress.

A film-horse, Champion, Crin Blanc,
    His mane in flames, tail smoking,
Furious at the awkwardness of world.

Hurt, impatient, apprehensive, wild:
    Bringing out all his flags. All froth
And stallion-fire and stamping hooves.

So vulnerable. So much bigger
    And more powerful than you
You have to whisper, trying to call

Him into himself. As if you could!
    He'll maybe never say –
Or anyway not now – exactly what rule's

Been broken. Like making lunch
    For an angry child
To take to school.

He doesn't feel you're on his side.
    You don't know how he'll be
When he opens what you've made

But you pick the freshest bread you have,
    Damp ham with lettuce, add a Coke,
A Cadbury's Egg, and Pringles, anything you can

To get it back for him –
  That confident, look-what-I've-got,
Now-I-can-forget-about-her pride.

THE YAKS

... and never tell you

How I'll never see
Or partly see

The yaks
Descending the tree line,

First as spots on flat
Emerald, then their own buttocks

Lurching above them at sunset
Under the felt-sacks

Of salt, fur, charcoal,
Down to the Tsang-po river.

Piebald yaks, dun, sable, ginger –
Their amber and vanilla steaming eyes

Finding the way home as I never will
Through the fat tufts

[*Something something* . . .]
Steady the tilt

Of their horns
Over creamcurds of froth

In the rapids – this fallout
Of infamous rocks.

Look. Lean out and touch them –
There in the pale-face fjord

Where girls on the bank
Still tugging their shoes off

Yodel an evening song
To a bamboo flute.

Exactly this song
For a faraway lover.

JAVA

Suppose that yesterday
The face you most want to see beside you
    Turned up all over the papers.
Just, say, a bit of it, smile and eyes
Throwing out front page over the masthead logo,
    That lisp of a look that thrills your heart

To bits. You'd be jolted, wouldn't you?
All day he's lying doggo
    On doorsteps, careening through the Tube.
Why are copies of the bloody thing still hanging about
    Imbued with the swamp fluorescence

Of late-night Safeways, next to *Esquire*?
The headline could have been 'World War'
    Or 'Rift with Mars'
For all you saw. But today
    They're throwing him away. Deadwood. Lumber

For recycling. He can come to you now.
File him sixty-nine times over if you like –
    Or three, best number for sudden gift: see under
Stravinsky's humming birds
Who lit on him in exile. 'They settle
    On my hand. Axtlel. Celesto. Java.'

The moment you say it, whispering, surprising the hell out
Of both of us, I imagine you falling
Through wall to wall rain – the tears
   Of a thousand grandmasters
As Kasparov gets beaten by machine – to the blue
Of your bedroom as you dream, one day, it'll be,

And dream of showing me. There you go
Through the dark, aflare in your parachute *de luxe*.
Origami in white flame, a billion crumpled sparks
   To every square. Is that all there is to hold a man
When he lets go and trusts to the sky?
A mushrooming ton of mad cream –

Quicksilver, aiming to liquefy behind itself
As atoms do inside a caterpillar
When it settles its shoulders into the chrysalis,
   Spinning harness for a resurrection hammock
Soft-skeined as sugar-cones they give to brides in Cairo,
And offers itself to sleeping-beauty work?

Here you are anyway, for real,
Holding me up on your thighs, with that lava-flow
We know as city moonlight
   Pasting neon, nitrogen,
And old stars
Round the room. Whispering into my collar-bone,
'I can be silent, with you.'

And my heart decides to be a helium balloon,
Molecules legging it, lighter and lighter
To a lunar rumba: all that helium, second in
   The Periodic Table after hydrogen, escaping,
Joining Deep Blue and the mystical .02
Per cent of the stratosphere.

One day you'll be mineral, be ash,
All this warmth and strength I'm joined to.
But not now. Not yet. And not if I can help it.
   As you're coming down to earth,
'Blue Velvet' syruping away on tape, I'm cradling
This blue-white moss you call your hair

Against my jugular, my skin. So tearable, the silk
Men trust their bodies to.
The world below us tilting
   In a drift of Chardonnay: coffee shares up,
All the world stocks of coffee-beans hammered
By frost in Brazil, the dolphins whistling alarm

To the tuna in a dawn concerto, sea freezing
To a rhinestone wave, dangling albino snakes
Of hi-tech foam. And the sun's become a black balloon
   Three centimetres off the horizon
But not giving, never giving up
On generosity. Some turnaround has come. Chess

Will never be the same. As if we heard words from our
Own language, something we belong to, suddenly
On a radio in Kazakhstan,
   Mid-negotiating a meal, a bed,
A no-hope Visa card. We're landing
Our joint enterprise, our parachute-cum-helium,

At a hill-shrine: a little pyramid of tiger-sticks
That looks like nothing on earth. So ordinary
You never find the path here when you try.
   Hibiscus blossom, staggered reeds, bamboo.
Ribbons and mirrors fluttering from
The lowest branches. You don't know what they mean

But someone rates this place enough to hang them here.
You step across the boundary you didn't spot
And wow – you're in. Together. The sacred precinct.
   Can't do a thing
About it. We've been around. But suddenly here's you –
Who never stop talking, ever, your mix of nerves

And Mr Uppity, anguish on over-drive, tenderness, pride
And wonder, trusting-to-luck and asking-for-more,
Plus asking-for-sympathy chaos – and me
   Whom I can't describe, belly-flopped in
To whatever you call this place. A jungle shrine
On a stripped-pine floor. A deep-sky blue.

You want it to live for ever,
This body you wonder at. You want to open
Ribs and breastbone
In fleshy Lycra wings

And fold him, hold him safe in
That red-feather home. You can't imagine
This body you adore will die. In fact,
You know it won't. You know he's afraid

Of losing that lord-of-the-jungle way
He thinks he's got to do things.
Order the drinks. Write cheques. Drive cars.
You'd like to be there, ease what's coming

When he's in disguise as old.
And show him how your body, down
To its blue-varnished toes, still glows
From touching his.

. . . how I imagine
It'll always be like this. Even when my soul's
A shadowless blue ark
Headed for the place where shadows stop

And crowded with painted animals,
Panda, giraffe, that shelduck tossing in the bows,
The bubbly lion and donkey, doused
In the billows of the St John Passion:

Its lavish dog's-tooth paintwork
– All the Dulux colours, Prussian Blue,
Mongolian Forget-Me-Not –
Skimming out to sea for ever,

Ever (can you credit it?)
Away from you. But somewhere
In an inner locker
There'll be the accident black box

Recording this midnight hunt of yours
For buried treasure:
A song you want to give,
However insensitive I've been.

And still at the end
(Whoever's first)
If the ember-light has gone,
We're not in breathing distance

Of each other, lives went
Down different alleys,
I'll see
You naked here like this.

Rembrandt-intimate and free
In the small glow by my bed.
The painter's way to get across
The glow you made my life, and me.

*

UNDERWATER

They never knew where he was –
Pickled every evening by five,
Prowling fierce and convivial
Down the tottery backstairs –

And still don't, even here
With tubes down him
To his duodenum.

She'd like to reach her hand
Across the cities – a stem
Of coral with green leaves on it –
And provide a bowl

Of silverberries
Glowing five colours at once,
Or red jelly laughing-beans

To the small wild man
In hospital at last,
Smouldering under sedation –
Bugger this for a lark –

And letting go
His renal system, his left lung.
Taking pride in smiling

At the surgeon still
With half a face.
And a lipoma,
A greedy mahogany udder

Sucking like a puppy:
A sea anemone
Under his sawed-through jaw.

BALKAN

She's supporting her torso
In the grey plastic chair
  Of a clinic in Psychicho.

Tape to her nose tips oxygen down
To the contused lung
  And a plaque of cement thumps 'tomb'
On her chest through cortisone haze
In dialect of Thirties Marseilles.
  At three, the physiotherapist

From Missolonghi
Peckers layers of tissue
  Over her heart

While I get rung up by the Embassy painter,
Wanting to limn
  (Yes, he actually says it)
My chestnut hair and blue eyes.
I have brown hair, green-muddish eyes
  And a friend

Drowning in a chair
In the vanilla dust of Psychicho.
  Plus an Embassy

Stamping unicorns and lions
On the crust of Crème Brûlée
  At the Ambassador's
'Britain in Athens' Festival
He hopes will get him a K,
  With a Serbian flatiron.

A DRINK IN THE NEW PIAZZA

(*In Memoriam Gerry McNamara*)

(i)

They were switching on headlights
Through A40 dusk, despite
The blaze from Mister Lighting

And a glow-worm trek of aeroplane
Through the scuffed cloud.
A written line, a last letter

Running left to right
Of the flyover
Till it smudged out in coughs,

The little source drawing south
Away from its end: that soft
Broken run of cotton commas.

(ii)

Driving west, I took
Your sea-grass stairs with me. As if,
If I kept them accurate
You wouldn't go.

Perivale. Wycombe. 'Nearly New Cars'.
On all of them I laid
Roan tiles from your kitchen
With its open garden door,

A house with a white inside
And a green-gray shirt on the floor

Of a bathroom tessellated blue,
A master-design in Ming
For you – who knew the entire score
Of *The Sound of Music*

And didn't want to be cremated
Because it just might hurt.
Who'd asked me to your funeral
Before you died, to sing.

(iii)

By some miracle you pulled, my breath –
Choked in London flu as well as tears –
Did soar up the ribs of St Saviour, more

Or less as it was meant to do,
Beyond where you were lying,
Not on the sofa of your late-night den

With its driftwood press
And Allegro, Allegro, Largo,
In a box that had not a thing to do with you.

(iv)

The earth bit was worst
And you'd thought of that too
When you vetoed Dido's *Lament*
('Too sad'). The thud of lilies
That could only be
The thud of lilies, nothing else –
Or the first shot of *Dr Zhivago*.

The mound of pinkish clay
Against those tungsten hills,
And two hefty men
Walking away from it, back to HQ
After a good half-day,
Swinging from post-sacramental torsos
The straps that lowered you.

(v)

But Gerry, the way you held
All of us, two or three hundred, close
All day!

The way you went
On All Saints' Eve, telling everyone
Through the mobile phone

It was alright, you were OK,
It was like a new city, something of Rome
But narrower. You could half see

The mazy streets. As if you'd registered
At twilight and were on the brink
Of going out, checking your jeans carefully

For change – ducat, piastre,
Rouble – and passport, Visa card, your hotel key,
For a drink in the new piazza.

Ruth Padel's passionate new collection is a woman's eye view of a love affair, with darker undercurrents of mortality and loss. Shifting between vulnerability and guilt, trust and doubt, tenderness and frustration, reproach and the exaltation of deep love and sexual happiness, Padel's extraordinarily bold, intimate book explores the risks and complexities that go with falling in love.

Wonderfully versatile in tone, it blends the lyrical and the colloquial, formality and wit, myth and the Spice Girls. It includes the poem that won the 1996 National Poetry Competition 'Icicles round a tree in Dumfriesshire' ('A daring blend of fire and ice, passion and design' – Jo Shapcott).

Ruth Padel lives in London. This is her fourth poetry collection.

'If Wallace Stevens and Anna Akhmatova were one and the same person, you'd have Ruth Padel.' Paul Durcan

PRAISE FOR *FUSEWIRE*

'Rich, haunting lyrics.'
Time Out

'A refreshing marriage of intelligence and sensuality.'
Sarah Maguire, *Kaleidoscope*

'Dantesque, impressive and desolating.'
Bernard O'Donoghue, *Independent*

CHATTO POETRY

£7.99

Cover painting:
Rembrandt, Girl at a window
by permission of the trustees of
Dulwich Picture Gallery

www.randomhouse.co.uk
Chatto & Windus, Random House, 20 Vauxhall Bridge Road, London SW1V 2SA

ISBN 0-7011-6715-7

9 780701 167158

Rembrandt Would Have Loved You